ISBN 9781976115165

editors: levi bentley and jonathan hamilton

Cover: Gabriel William Price-Staller, Untitled
2015, crayon on paper. 8.5 x 11

Warehouse Productions
Philadelphia, PA

Submit to:
boneless (dot) skinless (at) speakwright (dot) org

boneless skinless

Excerpt from **THE ALLOMOTHER & THOSE WHO COVER HER**

(a single section of the book-length serial work *Sousveillance Pageant*)

Sousveillance Pageant is currently enrolled in a mandatory online training course, offered by the University of Phoenix, called "Title IX for Life: Understanding the Legal Sanctity of the Body through the Lens of Corporate Liability." The class is a profound exercise in cross-institutional hierarchical deflection. Several years back, the managers of the small business where Sousveillance works began to fear they were focusing too much on people's actual sensations and lived experiences of sexual violation and not enough on the company's susceptibility to lawsuits. Doubtful of their own capacity to take responsibility for such nuances, the managers elected to outsource the task, downsizing the costs associated with such trainings via the bulk enrollment of each and every currently active employee.

As a form of education, Sousveillance has, in all honesty, found the training course to be acutely demoralizing. "How is it," she wonders aloud from her cubicle, "that only my utterly isolated online participation can qualify as recognizable preparation in this realm?"

Individual employee performance evaluations take the form of periodic clickable test questions appearing on each person's standard-issue desktop computer monitor. If Sousveillance answers any of these multiple-choice inquiries incorrectly (including in the form of "over-response" or, in other words, if she thinks something described is more sexist than the curriculum believes it to be), she has to start all over, with a new scenario, with different multiple-choice options, but the same end goal of avoiding legal liability. Ultimately, what each person is being tested on is extremely narrow in scope: Do I know how to "appropriately" position myself so that the institution cannot and will not be sued?; Am I confident in my capacity to say the "right" things in order to prevent potential litigation? All other responses are coded as "wrong" even if and when they might be understood as ethical.

So far the biggest perk of Sousveillance's long-distance enrollment has come in the form of free access to the University of Phoenix's limited database of e-books and audio files. The collection is hardly stunning, but it includes an expansive online request system that the Pageant herself finds irresistible. Should an exact title be unknown to an individual, he or she can also request by genre, by topic, by academic discipline, or "by description." Availing herself of the "by description" option has become an important and frequent anti-depressive life tactic for Sous across the past four months.

Whether or not the Pageant ever subsequently receives the books that she requests scarcely matters (which is fortunate, since she rarely ever does); rather, it is the asking itself that provides the distinct and mood-buoying pleasure. Today, under the category of genre, Sousveillance types in "invention narrative." After another second of thought and before hitting "enter," she adds the word "failed" in front of "invention" and then just as quickly deletes it. She begins dutifully filling out the description field, offering forth a level of detail that rapidly extends far beyond the suggested maximum word count.

DESCRIPTION OF TITLE:

This is the origin story of a thing that was actually made. If the text has been properly catalogued, it shall be found under non-fiction. It relays the history of a 3rd grade child's creation of a "self-tipping hat" for her elementary school science fair. To construct her invention, the child uses one of those giant foam novelty hats —frequently purchasable at large venue sports matches— as the base armature and installs an orange terrycloth sweatband inside its brim. The elastic band stretches extensively when prompted to do so by the forward thrusting of its wearer, and then reluctantly "springs" back into place post-maneuver.

If "springs" is arguably an optimistic verb choice, then the claim of "self-tipping" is also arguably a tad exaggerated, given that the invention requires the girl to fling her head with great gusto in the direction of the addressee, at which point the foam hat swells and flops before the receiver's eyes, then returns, staggering, to its prior position. To be frank, the invention does not so much save its user a gesture as it replaces one gesture with another. However, it does subtract the greeter's need to ever engage the fingers in the project of acknowledging another in greeting. The mechanics, it must be observed (and unfortunately for the girl, it is keenly observed by the science fair judges) are far from graceful, almost to a degree that makes it unclear whether each and every addressee will necessarily register the salutary move as the unequivocal demonstration of welcome and respect that is intended.

Despite the growing number of onscreen notifications insistently warning Sousveillance that she is over-filling the "description" entry box beyond its capacity, she adamantly continues:

```
The volunteer school board, whose members have been
recruited to serve as the science fair judges,
are divided on whether the young girl's invention
reasonably counts as "science" and if so, why. There
is a quiet dispute that occurs near the snack table,
heavily laden with double-crème Oreos and tiny
paper cups of poorly prepared Crystal Light. The
accompanying diagrammatic posterboards which the girl
has painstakingly created to provide context for her
"innovation" each feature drawings of the traditional
but "arcane" "finger-driven" method of hat-tipping,
brutally stricken through by bright-red markered Ø
Ø Ø signs and a near hysterical rainbow stream of
accusatory exclamation points.

The girl does not win a prize. Truth be told, she and
her peers have rarely had contemporary cause to tip
a hat at anyone; indeed, the question of what has so
obsessively directed the girl's attentions to the
automation of this task in particular is shrouded in
mystery. The girl has never seen an older man in a top
hat anywhere except on Sundays on the Turner Classics
TV channel.

But no matter. All morning and all afternoon she
stands there, in the stifling hot elementary gymnasium,
exuberantly hoisting her head forward and allowing the
over-sized gear that is perched there to leap back
imperfectly, but not without a certain grandiosity,
onto her noggin. Her accoutrements are clownish, but
the girl is absolutely solemn. She faces each board
member squarely and offers each one her finest demo.
```

"Please," Souveillance writes in the final NOTES area, "I need to know everything I can about that girl! No reference or resource is too small. No mention too negligible or too intangible! Thank you." The Pageant pushes the enter button with great zeal, and then pushes it again, at least four times more, for good measure.

Sousveillance knows that in all likelihood this will turn out to be just one more essential reference material that she is unable to acquire. But still the request itself feels important; it serves as a means of bringing about the girl's temporary visibility within the grand catalogue of recorded being, if only via the sheer force and volume of the Pageant's desire.

The late poet and essayist Audre Lorde has written that "we fear the very visibility without which we also cannot truly live."[1] It is a phrasing which certainly rings true in relation to how frequently we as individuals are persuaded to secretly or silently bear inside of us those realities (be they joys or agonies) which if collectively spoken and acknowledged might bring a palpable measure of relief, understanding, or previously impossible openness to the dynamics of current conditions and relations.

If we concede that to be addressed is, in some sense, to be (or, at the very least, is one of its primary features), there is still the dizzying breach of all those dissonant experiences that follow in tow with *being.*

> To be addressed is to be seen (recognized by others for qualities you also recognize in yourself).
>
> To be addressed is to be rendered hyper-visible, to be registered (in reference to elements you don't have the luxury or the perceived credibility to determine).
>
> To be addressed is to answer to a name with which you identify (the laughing tilt of the head in the direction of a friend's annunciation).
>
> To be addressed is to be required to answer to a name with which you do not identify (the sharp cringe of the shoulders in recoil, even as the head turns in mandatory deferral).
>
> To be addressed is to be credited for one's efforts or honored for one's acts (to receive a unique and personal accolade).
>
> To be addressed is to be called out or fingered for blame, to be painted by an act of criminalizing transference (while the one who paints or points or calls out enjoys a royal and blanket impunity).
>
> To be addressed is to be scolded, to serve as a mere foil for the delivery and reception of someone else's idiosyncratic pet peeves, newly re-sleeved in the false form of "general truths."

---

1   Lorde, Audre. *Cancer Journals,* Aunt Lute Books, 2006.

To be addressed is irrepressible.
We crave it or we fear it, we seek it or we flee it, and still it happens.

> *I dressed up, hoping to avoid her recriminatory aura and nonetheless*
> *still received a stern, infantalizing dressing down.*

> *I fessed up, seeking to gain his confidence and was first dissed, then summarily*
> *dismissed.*

> *I messed up, calling out over and over "hey you!" instead of "hey me!"*
> *"hey we!" "hey oh-so-many ghosts of Caesar!"*

> *I pressed my nose against the glass seeking traction, aiming to act*
> *as a witness, but was blessed only with the misty imprint of my own obfuscating*
> *fog.*

Not even a dog's tailwag flagged me down in acknowledgement.

And this message too was clear. To not be recognized, to be refused all address, also does its damage; it constitutes a critical and brutal component of both past and present traumas. These traumas affect society directly through an individual's experience and indirectly through the collapse of social structures. The resulting implosions wreak havoc not only on our own erogenous zones–our lonely pulses of yearning and love and hatred–but on the ozone as well.

In other words, it is not merely "individuals" who suffer from a subsequent inability to regulate stress; who succumb to reactive, aggressive states in their plaintive efforts simply to be seen; who fall into the trap of variously internalizing their own capture or erasure along the intentionally razored fracture lines of race and class and gender. It is whole nation states that do and that do so dutifully, as if it was an act of loyalty to cultivate and amplify these reverberating cycles of psychic and physical harm, rather than to warm the waters against them.

As if it was a matter of patent honor to leave behind for others this toxic fodder of inter-generational paranoia: the foible of roiling panic defenses and electrified fences gone blotto. Whose densely embroiled footprints are sloppy, heaving, turbid, oozing. They linger and stew long after the incipient events and sentient non-events that launched them have passed. They are material and historical, as well as emotional.

DDT may have been banned from all public use in 1972
but it is still found in 55% of American bodies.

in paper thin bodies
in bodies that persist on paper only
in bodies down to the wire
in wired bodies
in undercover bodies
in bodies under covers

under blankets, under sheets,
under lease contracts, under easements,
under the uneasy weight of heavy garments

in bodies clad in nothing more than undergarments

Situated in an ungarnished glass display case at the 2013 Venice Biennale was an exhibition providing the viewer with a different window into how subjectivity could be at once manipulated, sublimated, and painfully pulled apart in response to the very same exposure-time issue (call it a "photographic problem" or a "photographic opportunity") that the earliest police mugshots had made manifest. In long, narrow, wooden viewing boxes, the artist Linda Fregni Nagler had arranged a collection of almost 1,000 images under the title of *The Hidden Mother.* In picture after picture, taken between 1840 and 1930, the female caregiver is intentionally eclipsed, shrouded, or scratched out in order to foreground the centralized child who nonetheless still requires a matriarchal anchor in order to endure the process of image-burning,

in order to learn how not to squirm.

Whether said clumpy berms of looming female furniture should register to today's viewer as humble or obscene, they can certainly be seen as a pinnacle illustration, replicated ad nauseam, of the gendered nurturer as an essential but devalued buttress, an anonymous stabilizer, an invisible pillar of support.

Or perhaps we should say, visible, but intended to be ignored

cordoned off until the body is transformed
into a boldly disappeared oddity
a fraudulent storage unit tuned to care for others
even at the glaring cost of her own smothering

just another smothered mother   multiplied a thousandfold
both folding the sheets and sordidly folded into them

As art critic Federico Nicolao notes, "They are subtracted from the meaning of the photographs while helping to create them, cancelled out so that the focus is on another subject."[2]

Rejected.   Made blank.   Blanketly erased.

Stationed as a corpus of pseudonymous corpses

To be addressed is to live at another's behest, to receive orders
the mordant body garbled by its cumbersome garbs
its anatomy having become a lumpen upholstery
that serves as a puppet holster for boasted-over offspring,
a springboard for the newborn's burgeoning class status.

A visual lattice work of profoundly delicate
and profoundly indecent poses

---

2 "The Hidden Mother" by Linda Fregni Nagler, *Harper's Magazine,* August 2013.

A glowing focus that ruthlessly rubs the viewer's nose in what it purports to disappear.

A form of deceitful optical steering preceded by millions of corollary antecedents.

For instance, when the Asian American documentary filmmaker Loni Ding sought, more than a century after its occurrence, to cinematically tell the story of the transcontinental railroad's construction here in the United States, the existing archives presented her with a singular conundrum. While Chinese workers had accounted for 90% of the monumental labor of blasting and hand drilling thirteen tunnels through the solid granite of the Sierras, they had been systematically eliminated from all photographic records of those efforts.

Said workers had been employed by the Central Pacific railroad company who was responsible for building the route east from Sacramento, California, while Union Pacific worked west from Omaha, Nebraska. The two tracks converged at Provo, Utah in 1869. And when they joined, a celebratory commemorative moment was staged to capture the hammering of the final "golden spike" that marked the route's completion. This widely published photograph featured dozens of purported "track workers," all facing the camera, without a single Chinese visage among them.

In Ding's own documentary, this legendary photo also appears, but before our eyes it is gradually transformed, using a rudimentary photoshop trick whose apparatus is purposively made visible to the viewer. A slow, computer-generated graphic substitution unfolds on screen, ultimately replacing 90% of the men featured on the Central Pacific side with images of Chinese workers: a transparent "doctoring" of the image which Ding performs with insistence and with admiration for those whose portraits she inserts.

What, after all, was the original image if not also "doctored"?

Its "real" people presented in "false" poses
unrepresentative of their actual roles in history
or in the community.

Which picture, ultimately, is more fake and which more authentic?
Which better reflects a genuine lived history and which only its contrived
mimicry?

Is *either/or* even useful here or perhaps only *both/ and?*

When asked to explain her choice of visual alteration, Ding replied: "It is a way of combining research history with fictive storytelling. Fundamentally, we are finding ways to create a first-person voice using historical and cultural materials in which the personal accounts and experiences of Asians in America are conspicuously absent."[3]

A way to muscle forth the precious remains of a once robust
presence from a dispersed field of fleeting gestures
and material tatters

When it comes to the matter of established public perception
or comprehension, the physical nerves, rods, and cones
of the eye itself are always available on partial loan
to the day's prevailing ideological mythologies.

When the occasional Victorian scholar arrived at the Venice pavilion to peer in at Linda Fregni Nagler's sweeping panorama of "hidden mothers," they saw something that was both the same as and different from what you and I saw. They challenged other viewers in their circumference to consider how these poorly hidden human armatures might have registered in the past, not as a morbid spectacle, but as celebratory evidence of a child's aliveness. These scholars reminded those who would listen how the startlingly high rates of infant mortality meant basically that posthumous portraits were taken for the norm, requiring a veritable swarm of ostentatious and stylized hints to persuade the intimate onlooker otherwise.

What we perceive today as awkwardly ominous and macabre, a person potentially looked at then, and was flooded with relief at the manifold proofs of goofy vivaciousness.

The distance between dead wrong and dead on can be so slight
sometimes. Or so giant.

Just another pliant gap through which you miss the whiffs
of your own prejudices and presumptions.

---

3 Excerpt from "Documemoir Visual Approach" by Loni Ding.
http://www.cetel.org/docu.html

Emily Abendroth

THE SYSTEM

Book covers
curl, shaker

caked with salt
humidity—

I can't speak for
thinking of you

St. Francis, hand
aloft in the garden

here you are here you are here you are

My daughter collects buttons in a box
whose only purpose is containing them
while their purpose is being contained.

X-ing out the window panes,
collecting non-perishables

watching it rain in the ocean.

Kate Colby

RED EYE

What is water's natural state—
ice, gas or liquid?

How did it first appear and
does this answer the question?

More or less is a measure
of quality, give or take

of quantity, history
isn't what it used to be—

the idea of life
outliving itself

fruit flies orbit black
bananas on the counter.

Kate Colby

MONS PUBIS

you have the most
beautiful ideas
by your mind i am
relieved of
wondering after
scurry or slamming
on the concourse
my bag into legs
now my sack of
action
i rest my cheek on
your shoulder bone
ledge for this
face of mine
the first midnight
i fisted
someone
my grandmother is a god to me
i mean i pray to her
to keep my sister ok
biking daily the
brooklyn bridge
or there there's
a pretty brain bone
all spent up
can the dead
protect the living
in our heads
illusion
i refuse to discard
like spent pens
and sun times

it could be exciting
to blow a new roof
but i can't quite
tell what we
are to do to
each other
you seem both
willing and resistant
so i peek around
the strand of
tracks
mons pubis
sacrum skyward
how i dance now
how you sit
it disperses
your power
renegotiates it
on a train
the effect
multiplied
by pace

Emma Brown Sanders

RELEASE FANTASY

i have been waiting for
my life to be less marvelous
tapping along like my sneakers
are stage lights shining up my thighs
so everyone sees me crush cans and grin
i have been eating a piece of pie for days now
strawberry rhubarb
which the man stacking
takeout boxes called a shrubbie
i didn't want to throw it away
the pie made from this sugar and that
which went down like
a shock to a bitch thin as a syringe
the use of "bitch" here is distracting
it takes one from the point which is
caloric intake and its
legislation on signage
right. so my marvelous life
it was getting a little thick
neural pathways become
accustomed to cellular starvation
and in fact demand it
under chemical intake
the stage lights went up some watts
burning my legs and turning
my vagina a ghastly blue
i wanted to send you a warning text
the flight attendant said *airplane mode*
the flight attendant said *our approximate*
time in air will be four hours
four minutes and four seconds
that's how accurate we are today

the flight attendant said *ALL RISE*
and seemed to really enjoy that
my blue vagina was murmuring
quick as in prayer or crazed in
a park reciting my *vital demystified art*
to echo
to drug alley
to driftwood
and geese shit
in bed there was a river
behind my eyes
i felt fairly certain
i was a stone fence
you were disassembling
and reassembling in blue
the only other color
on my person was
a credit card
i said, this must be love
because nobody knows
a self-sustaining organism like bliss
the TSA fucked up my vibrator
it was really a rattle then
and would no longer bring me
to tears which was the only time i wept
the woman with vista
dumped wisdom which
was more like a doorstop
i resolved to stop
impaling myself on
self-presentation like
the better i look the worse
i'm doing
who you are is important
how you write is not important
what you wear is the most important
i didn't believe the cascades
because some were snowy
and some were not
this seemed inconsistent
and the clouds concurred
and conferred
to cover the mountain range

i felt satisfied as on
the telephone giving
one and a half stars
to a place i'd never been
just tapping between
the middle of two stars
so nothing actually happens
your horse rode up
and i cried riderless, HA!
i was like all good decreationists
reading simone
absorbing her as
she would have abhorred
my joints gleaned
how to separate out self
not to give it up
but to let it perch
on an outstretched limb
marveling
simone said *that's not really what i meant*
marguerite porete said *you're such a little slut*
i WAS feeling whoreish
my spirit hanging out at men
standing very still in liquor stores
standing behind the register
staring out at the mountains
which were behind clouds
which were behind buildings
which were behind glass
which sometimes got broken
the man was the glass picker-upper
his gaze was like a window
i was the white bitch beaming up
your horse had no head then
i thought oh god
i don't know you at all
really i was jealous
you'd found your own
with whom to cuddle
though that word seemed
to me to barf a little
maybe it's recompense
for walking just

who i was into a household
someone had given me
an earthly accoutrement or two
which is a very pretentious
way of saying young
and well-breasted
and these facts walked around
with me all day like
i ought to make
a bound volume of them
killian says anarchy's
just believing that
no one should
ever be in charge
i can't even reign
over my own facts
instead i instagram plants
and fake giggle
with the bourgeois
who let me sleep
in their big bed
i got stoned and
saw a song in my head
about seeing god
in a tree and a street
then i felt once more
i'd swallowed you
so my chest was
beating double
i climbed over my
seatmates who were holding
each other and sleeping
then i REALLY hated myself
i prayed on the page
because it is slower
there than a brain
especially a brain
on a plane
in the hotel
i felt my skull throb
which said clearly
it wanted it to end
you deliver to me

a kind of stakes
that are very dangerous
so i like it and lick
your photo on my telephone
and you taste
just like my finger smear
it's nutritious
when i was hungover
i was certain
i'd forget you sober
and when i was sober
i fucked myself up to feel you
it went on like this
the takeout box
i couldn't toss
and the syringe
bitch shock of shrubbies
the cleverness of indulgences
is each one's ending
that's what gets us begging
i ingested every
well-done love song
i have really immaculate
taste in insanity
i mean i do it WELL
shine a light on and all
someone asked me
questions and
i inked the answers
all over my hand
it came out just
like a ball and chain
i became more broad and soft
which is to say womanly
but could still
punch a playground's
lights out, eyes shut tight

Emma Sanders

SILENCE IS PUNISHMENT

for Art Farm

(Because) better than does not equal enough.

Rather wander / rather fixate.
By car instead of plane.
Apart. A body.

Quarry

The mother who drove the daughter
and the daughter's boyfriend
because she doesn't know what else to do.
Better to be involved. In accumulated water.

Mother scared of this boy
and the whole world of boys.
What they will do.
Smile as if she doesn't see, until forced.

Like right now, she can turn her head
swim further,
the water easing,
so she doesn't have to hear it either.

Her timing is right. Far enough away
before he asks her girl, "Do you love me?"
She escapes the reminder—
how the echo starts so young.

Women Driving Men

Cholas: the kind of Mexican I will never be.
The hair, the lip liner, the pride in the chin.
Resurrected from old movies, and midwest remixed.
Gorgeous.

While their men lean back,
playing cool in the passenger seat.
As if they aren't vulnerable.
As if they don't want to drive.

Two Tractors

The tractors are old.
Still. Move earth.
Can't reverse / stuck in forward
Here now. Here now. Here now. Tempered.

Lightning Storm

Interrupts the quiet,
expands the limitations.
The sky is falling
and I can not calm

in the field,
in this marvel
of a one room
constructed from pallets.

Crashing acoustics, wind shear,
and innate fear.
I want to know why
I still want it after.

Antique Mall

Vintage journal $10. Grandma's quilt $95.
Who's still alive? Who would even know to notice?
When even what we thought we saw wasn't what we saw.
That's not vintage, it's old.

It's Art

It is a cast of a man: newspaper, flour, water.
Now a layer of kerosene.
Despite—takes awhile to light.
Initially, the breeze fights the flame.

Marissa Johnson-Valenzuela

from ***DISORIENTATIONS***[1]

Your writing is mere dust in the urn of representation, black calligraphy that only becomes clear against a black page.

If only we could be traveling beyond the incomplete rendezvous of division and cohesion rather than be drifting within it, then we might simultaneously light the edge of the paper and carry its warmth before the ring of the ceremony comes undone.

The body, now offered, is on the table—that profound space for gaudy vacillation, for awkward meetings, for remote nutrivity and visual interplay, for the pure instance in which tea takes on the perfect form of its teapot.

Language is a wandering tributary. How to describe the simple happiness that is to fish in its thick and irreducible ink? To look at, as in a magical elixir, its apprehended elements—a foreign word, fragmented sentences of guarded speech, an embarrassing utterance, filaments of what was written. And, here and there, a shimmer of the signifier.

Though your lexicon always has to find relief (and so be consumed) in cremation, the fire's kabuki-like rarity appears to sheath it—as the moon is enveloped, and figuratively cleansed, by the endless arms of space.

To be a poet is to open bent and undated mail not addressed to you.

What is the poem but a cupping and then scattering of grass, the somewhat amateurish breaking and flowering of emptiness?

For writing is precisely the act which unites the weightless things of the universe with a simple cut of the blade.

---

1 "Disorientations" collages together—and so "disorients"—two postmodern Orientalist texts: Kent Johnson's *Doubled Flowering: From the Notebooks of Araki Yasusada,* a yellowface simulation of hibakusha literature, and Roland Barthes's *Empire of Signs,* a semiotic treatise based on an invented system Barthes calls "Japan."

I have waited all week.

The gray chessboard of the sky
recomposed.

"It may be read,"
you told me, "according to the
long rhythm of the bodies
becoming skeletal."

In the margin of the mind,
seeing was diminished or denied
…something quietly
left a wake in dark water.

With chopsticks,
you set down in front of me
a flake of sound
pregnant with praxis.

In the background,
remains another background,
a somewhat windowed tableau.

You said, "Indeed,
space is not,
as you thought, a series
of numerous containers."

By then, I was covering
the formal chambers of my poem
along with its mournful frame.

Even so,
you said to me: "In the first half
of your original stanza
there is a definition of memorial
destined to be undone."

in the dream
the fascist counts
the open graves

"one, two, three, four…"
but it is useless

in the hall of his hotel
there are, strangely enough,
sounds of a barber

later, over his motionless hand
a moth fans its wings

à quelle heure ?
nan ji ni ?

last September is there

stuttering

in the clear heart of the

water clock

le rendez-vous

the schoolgirl mentioned to the self-absorbed monk

something about the difficulty

of dragging geometry   through the abnormal air

[UNDATED]

Here something hollowed out
and bottomless reveals its essence:
a wad of air
              frozen with the rose-wood fervor of 1945.

Crystallized in grease,
this emptiness is produced
in order to echo the river's stagnant smile,
to dry
        the milk of paradox
from within.

      For passages to branch
from traditionally silent
translations,
              the pink paper in the brown envelope
would have to dream beyond the minor cruelty of meaning.

Translation, you see, is a living lubricant,
a fact all the more provocative
in that the clock, face-down
      and running backwards,
recovers—as if with a long, calligraphic pin—
the bloody perforations of the hour.

Then the terror, lightly diluted,
is immediately soaked up
by the mud of Ujina Bay,

and the constructed question,
even if unrelated,

will conclude in lace.
When scattered, the golden flower
scrapes the oily substance of its maternal sheath.

Here, we gather numerous erasures by the ladle—

    as if they were carried forth by a density of sounds
pushing an illegible death-date through
the interstice of our wounds.

This scene is of Hiroshima
       as a purely audible object:

the crease of being
"photographed"
by the bombing,

       the 1, 2, 3
of   fritter,   fry,   *Inferno.*

Michael Leong

WHAT GOES ON IN THE HADRON COLLIDER

If, to make it, you gutted a mountain (builders
and scientists and those you paid to feed them
both), to blast and scoop and scrape until
the rock was paper skin on a dark lake

of dust, and if you commanded that they forge
inside the cavern a machine five leagues long,
so vast in its armature, so tight in its organs
that it could only be built by its own brittle self

as they watched, and if when the instruments
finished they yoked themselves to their creation,
they began to fire needle nose javelins of light—
crash test dummies in a cosmic pileup you hoped

would give off a certain kind of never before seen
spark, which, if you had seen, you'd never know
you had, because we have no name for the scale
of its magnitude (except the opposite of magnitude),

no name for the span of its time (forever, deconfined,
or: it's all relative)—and then if you built an arcade
of robot mouths to perceive it for us, to spit
the kind of data our people can digest and they graphed

it to the next-to-next-to leading order and cried
"there's a bump there!" and the bump remained
after they calibrated the detector and after they asked
it the difference between a difficult calculation and a flash

of insight, and you are down four trillion dollars and we
are down a mountain and the evidence is unquestionable
because there's the thing you made the machine to make,
the thing you asked it to show you, the eye and the image

inside of it and all of us faint mirrors turning in the terminal dark.

Mai Schwartz

AUDIT

They say everyone in the dream is you: the dentist,
the tawny mutt you scooped from the median
on the way to his office, that red light shining
in your eyes forever, the man who picked up
when you dialed the number on the tag saying
there's no home for her here anymore, the car
filling with hair, your throat filling
with hair saying okay I am her home now
and forever, though who can say once
your lease is up. All contracts are subject
to revision. Your name could change
at any time and who should be notified
and what shall we send to the engraver
first. You fill cavities, you wait narrowly
on the median, shining and shining,
you roll your eyes when the phone
rings, there's no home here, no
one should be asking a thing
of you, why does the dog
look up darkly, why
flinch so much,
it's only
noon.

Mai Schwartz

so you never happened

/

so you ate your nascent organs under a tarp

/

this too
has a history

/

it's a question of some interest
I only wash my hands if
someone watches

/

this isn't where
I lost it
it's where
there's light
to look by

/

take this shrapnel
carbon date it

as if we needed proof

when the monster
divorces her pain
who will sign
for it? who
will testify?

/

how gauche
to be a perpetual
dissatisfaction
machine

to thrash
the podium
demanding
payment

there was
a contract
there was!

but to know
how it's kept

/

shall we worship the shine
in the floorboards

shall we say
it's time
for me to
shoulder
your violin

I am sawn
in half
like a girl
coffined
in a magic trick

stall me,
pretend

you don't
know that
everywhere
honeybees
die with
their stingers
intact

/

break every leg
in America, baby
stalk the quad
like you paid
for it in nerve
the cicadas have
called up their
reserves just
to fall around
you like brittle
grenades so
when the idiots
line up for a
diploma cut in
tell them to ride
their tragic
skins to the automatic
finale. look ma
I packed you
a bag: two shades
of lipstick, a pen,
ten crumpled bills
to tip the troll when
you're afraid, your
own heart's skilled
baroque devotions,
a matchstick,
one held note.
otherwise what?
what I know is
we are orphans
of what we
desire more
than what we've lost

Mai Schwartz

ROSEANNE IN *RUSHMORE*
(UPON HEARING THAT ROSEANNE "LIKES" TRUMP)

"Nihilo sanctum estne?"

The Mrs. Robinson I wanted   to build aquariams
for might as well have been you, Mrs. Connor(your daughter Darlene's
beauty not-with-standing)there was
your palimpsest of tenderness-brutality-tenderness

the way hearing the truth tosses off the hat
of everything else but it's also true that not all of your episodes
are available

      like human memory is selective
      hellbent for disappointment
      & one woman's wagon
      is another's sobriety

So this is just a record I can play when I want to remember
how it felt to know this particular loss.

ROSEANNE AS ANN WILSON OF HEART

They've been singing the same songs for years
& at least you can say you're not that
kind of celebrity/poet/one-trick pony

They say it takes one to know one,
as in what it is not to be on one side
or the other & going back & forth
& not seeing lines/seeing how far
we get from real bird sounds
sounding monologues of fury.

I heard you might resurrect,
which is a thing now: Revivals.
But Jesus or Buffy or any Cylon
will tell you, *Nobody comes back
the same*—which isn't really
about how they came back,
it's about how they never really were.

r/b Mertz

ROSEANNE AS MARIANNE ON *GILLIGAN'S ISLAND*

for Dan Shapiro

STOP picturing the spectacle
the grimace/face palm/face paint
joke of one appearing as an other
& imagine/know that we are
so far right on the spectrum
of optimism, in such a deserted
State that the sweetest girl nextdoor
is Darlene & the piteous mother/fucker
who daydreams us into a lottery heaven,
the one we murmer the name of
during our death scenes:::
Somebody said wouldn't it be funny
but poor daughters know how truth
is rich & rare like a diamond,
how telling the truth like an ass-hole
is kinder than all that rich reality syrup
of euphemism hiding who made
what you have with yourself,
or a dollar sign or a man

FIVE FORBIDDEN DANDIES FIGHTING IN THE WOODS WITH SWORDS: OR, LI HAUZ LIVRES NAH

"Il a hermites en ceste forest a qui on en fet heres."
—*Perlesvaus*, Anonymous

"I covered my head with my coat and I fled madly from this country of spells."
—"The Embalming Women," Marcel Schwob, trans. Kit Schluter

i. Dandy of Pleasure

I'm alive again from fights with roughnecks—
see me a… c-contrecoeur or w/e acting up an idiot with
someone else's swords—and not very sure
I'm saying that right—everybody's darling
in my frock, everybody collared
by my ringing lights. In sword land all hands
a wretched cop calling cop on one another
with coward alarums. O woe o woe, I swan
in and out of the dizzying awning
snatching up them golden bowls,
dashing them on the ground in a heavy snit.

I'm rich and richer every day,
I barely exist in my dream of leisure,
I'm slashing wildly, my feet don't touch
the floor. Dandy of Insolence whose name
I don't remember hurl urself at me, kill me,
tug at my mantle with teeth until
told by your own sweet dad what armor is.
Revise this night again again—I begin again
fidgeting with my frock in platinum.
I undo the chainmail. I get all feisty
about that plaster head floating up the white river
towards secret Byblos and spoil my appetite.

Innumerable gunshots in the night that are
none of my business, but I clasp hands
with the delivery boy anyway, hold him
in the domestic fold of my cape until
the buildings stop burning and the snipers turn to nap.
Little appetizers for hours,
my gilded dome, some made-up shit about spoils,
free drinks, a symbol of virtue kissin on itself.

Later, village coroners conclude definitively
I am not the vanished generalissimo,
the famous Dandy Who Walks Amidst Silver,
heave their widower shoulders,
rend the jewels from my heroic medals,
eat the fringe off my epaulettes,
schlep my raggy body back into the canal.

ii. Dandy of the Grail

Of course I remember the idiot cup,
I kiss it in my dreams, and sip from its contours
in the soft den of my private lunches.
I bought it so cheap, I took it outside
and cracked it in half for laughs.
I found it in the cathedral, which I have,
and hoisted it forever. I saw it only
through a haze of cheesecloth,
fleetingly, as milk seeped through it.
I saw it fade into darkness in a painting
when the paint-dad threw fits and tore
the footlamps from my happy rounds.
I saw it run flat in a 3D landscape.
I was beat up bad by army guys
for making mean comments about it
in the village square.
My husbands and my wives made it real as a trick
while sharpening knives in the knife store.
I fell for it again and again.
I saw the main guy's fingers close upon it.
I looked it up in an incognito tab
in case it was naked. I fill my mouth with ice
when I see its form in passing.
I wasn't raised to ask frivolous questions.

I fill it with cranberry juice
and pour it down my spine.
Sent my lazy friends aquesting
for it and paid dear for their blurry snaps.
Stretch out an idiot hand to the air—
take this thing, this thing, this thing,
this thing I drop and squander,
I don't know,
I forgot to notice.

iii. Hero Dandy Slain By The Coward Henry James

Pardon my violence loved ones, pardon pardon,
my wet hair unspooling from
a proud head like a leaden egg.
People say my plots don't make good time,
so I run 'em through, I carbinado the bums.
I turn their flanks to flank steak, something,
I don't know, I turn their adams' apples
to apple sauce. I pierce their unhappy cysts,
flinch, say ugh, what comes out, I say,
it looks like pizza sauce.

Here is what became of my little 13th century—
my chansons are lacking,
everybody is acting, uh,
what'd you call it, deranged,
and all the fine proceeders filing
past with severed knight heads for show
are ostentatiously anti-semitic,
in a weird way, are balding due to sin,
are struck upon the backs with pox,
and their Occitans is perfect.
I too am party to that permanent crack
on the burnished noggin—
my sorry head unspooling my own discursive dregs.
I get concierge mixed up with consigliere,
ask the wrong cretin where to wet my whistle
and wind caught up again in combat
with one thousand thousand enemies.
I'm whaled on by hooligans until permanently dead.
I wake up and spill hot tea on my throat
and am permanently dead.

Please believe me—I don't ever read the papers.
Another text from god this morning: *BOOK TO [sic] LONG.*
I do not wish to be read as apologia for crusading.

Brothers, um, permit me again the long sentence,
all the boys named like yachts appearing
one after the other, offering pearls to my fingers,
small monster skulls cut from soap to my mouth.
Let me explain to you who is marrying who
and why, for the last time. Peep how coy I
set my head of papyrus upriver in its urn
to be hassled with longspears,
abandoned by kids riding dirtbikes
in this blighted state's drainage basins,
gnawed up by dogs, all scooped out, surprise,
all packed with delicious candy.
I no longer dither about this kind of thing
but spend my days sleeping in,
pushing my jewelry deep down in my tummy,
writing mean rumors for my friends'
art catalogues. I think I'll die soon—circa nineteen-whatever, oh, whatever—
the maids pump their fists.
Everything else you can revise, revise
and never stop piling. These words I dizzy at,
glance down, and puke to consider.
I take them between my pulping teeth. I don't stop grinding.

I'll know the name of every fake rake
I invented to put swords to
each one close-identical
in twelve billion homonymous ballads—
Cowboy Tom and Donald Food, Barbara Guest,
The Rider, Frank "Katanas" Frobisher, Dandy
of the Coat Rack, Dandy of Storms—
all in their winding shrouds in cowboy villages,
the onlookers, I'll know about that.
This one goes out to all the books
I got absolutely Yelled At
for wrecking with my guilty hands—
no fencing in the dialogue,
no twilight in the plot,
an algae that resembles
and acts like an algae

spilling out from the cusps
of the town's most criminal cups
a picture of fighter guys
fighting in the library
I can point to, hey,
I made that thing—

iv. *Dandy Who Breathes Underwater With Ease*

So sick and tired of talking with the pagans rulers.
Never sick and tired of talking with the pagans rulers.
In the beginning the fields flowed over with rice wine
and our limbs stank. Like at the beginning of this combat,
clutching the pizza delivery man
as a gamey kind of scraggly shape
emerging as form out of not-form,
a hand inventing itself to fumble
for a light switch in the hot dark.
I can't believe those
pagans are at it again.
I can't believe it goes up and down,
that wavy knife,
and its *my* perforated bod
that leaks out so balefully,
etc. etc.,
and nobody in particular is cured of their ills
and thus the continued abating of the water is insured.

human breath underwater, anyway, it's like
fighting, just like fighting with swords—
you do it with your friends
when your king isn't looking
and in the end it lets you down
a hideous trick played by mammal lungs and
priestcraft, ok, and this one with his
eyes closed, called
The Dual-Wielding Backflip Into Perdition
I too ride with the Luxury Boys
over oil slicks and into lush lagoons
seeking pleasure in denial
Tokyo drifting into blank delight
as a diffuse glow announced in the
throttled instance of a grotto

as a thing that dwindles in its annunciation.
I lay my dumbass lip upon my Dandy of Oxygen,
I forget that normal thing of air.

this secret you learn about in
underwater church—what floweth out
you do not keep
when the grimy fishes floweth in
so sick of being pagan rulers, so tired
of this godforsaken water-upon-the-land

v. Final Dandy XIV

I dream of fake grandeur-- this world is currently full.
My wealth gone over to cutscenes, one million-
million tuff swains queued as if in love before
some one-armed chud with his lips bent backwards
thigh deep in this river, abask
in the fading guts of black bears, trees being dragged
from one point to another, etc.
vanishing into peril
appearing again frustrated and obscure

find me decked out in the same tacky red raiments,
included in the execrable Fouke Fitz Warin as
background color or fucking nonsense
the dandy at the end of geographic history, I mean,
a theoretical figure sitting on a material stump
in the middle of this earth's most useless forest

I remain the least canonical by consensus and elsewhere,
consistently, both brute and boor,
having cut off the heads of giants
to prove a point vaguely,
or fill five minutes of aimless grinding—

me the guy from those fake lais
who ate all other dandies before him
alone in the clearing with a thistle once more
a fine sabre between its teeth
whistling interminably

do you remember that Spicer bit about fighting forever

in armor?
it's expensive.
fireworks, permanently.
that's not what he said I don't think—
startled by the noise and never unstartled,
to let go of this pizza guy,
hurl this ruby sword into the sun,
for some reason,
wash one's own hands in clotted creeks,
like one fresh form can imprint upon another
without recompense, my sweet dandies all
corps a corps, forget
about it, never mind,
forgive the interruption, swain, swain,
have at thee please

Christopher Schaeffer

SLIT UP

you put pies in the house
to smell like buyers

live there; but pie attracts
kids and three take

a picture of themselves:
two honeybearing

the third on your bed
to blow 4th grade gram

up: when the house
goes, you and Lee take a walk in

the woods where you'll move
—vacation part of Philly

six miles up a road that
folks have been walking

as long as folks have
been here, trade route

turned to sideways avenue
it's mostly empty storefronts

but up by your new house
it's cute: half a block from

the holy grail Wawa: liquor store
and pizza shop, hair salon

the one bar stays open
but the other closes at nine

or ten, so by grow up
you mean head in for the

night like you always
wanted: you mean get busted

up by buying curtains: we are not
having this fight in an IKEA

you go over by the couches
I'll go sit on that bed

and this thing you think I
mean, are you looking

at my face, what does
my face look like: we're on

our balloon setting, our
vertical—be okay for me:

inlay on the counters in this
new shit, tiny in our old house

like I think I'll just
sit in the bathroom and

read for a while and
you're holed up in there: but

that's where I wanted to be
we are not having

this out in IKEA—I say
it at home and you laugh

and go into the bathroom
anyway, and out on the steps

E's already there and tells
me about her spinout Virginia

weekend in the cut: a yellow
lab booked it and

her car bust a car
but a trump / pence sign

broke both their falls
and hugged her windshield

it shredded the sign when they
went to pull her out

Davy Knittle

SNOT NOW

soup of the day's coming out
of me

starts stony, resists until its met
halfway and you can add in

all the carrots and whiskey
you want

people reading "all the whiskey
in heaven" picture bathtubs

then prohibition and tall hats
and then put

the past in heaven, which is logic
all that old whiskey fermenting

in heavenly rest area over the years:
wake up nearly under morning's stairs

or in its yard, like object transfer
is imperfect and you want to appear

in the restaurant but instead
you're in the bain-marie. we agree

on the brothiness today is, but
I taste potato and you don't

you're an optimist:
you seize on that old sofa

taking dead relatives' chairs to be
auctioned, buying the chairs of the

further departed, trading up
I'm wearing that plum lip balm

to hail you and the plain one
to say don't pet

Dan's over again, running lights at
the baseboard: the set up of his big ask

Chelsea's out of town
and he's letting us hold the ring

we're cleaning out the attic
tithing to be dry-eyed

how many questions are satisfied
by the "ask again later" of old yearbooks

everything is serious
you can make a monstrous tower

by putting cereal box
on another cereal box:

wheaties on kix on cinnamon life
until it's perilously elevated

commitment takes awful verb phrases:
sinking your teeth or digging in

pour it on means all of it: your effort
fermented like soymilk: everywhere you

went during the day where someone
could have put you on a map

could have shown up and found you
sitting in a room

could have guessed when you might
have stood and walked the hall to pee

I do that. guess you. and then I stop:
take a second departure:

first the kiss in the morning, then
the part hours later where I consent

to see you soon and do the work
other than tracing how your day

is parallel to mine, so far as we seek
features that don't like to touch

Davy Knittle

GIVEAWAY

come   slowly
comes   slowly
came   tracing
              a finger
              across his
              dresser
              his tempo familiar

but slower
than you prefer.

the bruise that flowers,

you
like it this way.

you come
harder this way.

              body of christ,
              you soak through the mattress.

Maryan Nagy Captan

From **INTAGLIO DAUGHTERS**

15

She lowers owlets into your arms as if they weren't complete without them

Day after day I composed rows of words which would

not speak to me. My nervousness mounted, amounted to

An enormous or insurmountable absence, punctuated by

dying. As they fall, the leaves guide themselves by light

When you left they were still children, not the fear

of adulthood but the unlikelihood, and the color we

describe (as she hears it in her head). An unrest we

cannot translate. As for the 'grand' in grandmother

I suspect her of reading. Of returning to beginnings

 Of receiving the allegorical. Loss would have us revert

to childhood, retrieving nonsense which was never non sense

Very vary quite unburied, despite culpability

I know how to stuff myself into the unsaid

She sews eyelets into your charms as if they weren't discretely anthems

The train is in fact a curtain air can turn

He set out in his grandfather's coat to magnify

friends, sanctify electric, a song born in a bean field

You left me your breath, called me your mist

I did my crying in private but showed up with eyes absent

and soundless. She pulled the red silk river inside

herself and then laid down beside the tree beings

The music was miscible, a perfect counterpart to language

She liked being in the same noun with kin, kept herself on a short breach

I said 'hi' like a poppy in a root cellar, implied

distance implanted between us so you might miss me

You said 'put me on the map' but what you really wanted

was to put yourself there: green tea, magenta tea, blue tea

To wane is a pact a certain stare can burn

Two roses in the dark, one black the other invisible

The name of the song is feminine but only for one night

He wore his body on his sleeve, strode amiably into any weather

Face peeled open, features abrupt, hailing a ferryman

You could say reverberation is a gallop, a multiplicity

of bewildering forms, sonorous hounds of spelling

But how to move between your words and your thoughts

Confiscation is the same angel at a desk from every angle

Let me be very clear about running out of letters

I wore none around my neck. We did not show our books in public

Remember this isn't about us, but only our outlines

heaven's own child, lured into a bread house

Blue closing of the park, that lack unprintable

A landscape has endless false endings

How to forestall, star before cart

Reclining in the middle of an ample face

Dormantly I sat where I could see you

aslant ignoring windows full frontal

smudged with streaks of cloud

Book as filament, cracks along the surface

of an oracle make a fine filigree tree

signed seasons, scrolled, feigned

I assign you a secret name I dare not pronounce

Maroon hemmed, potent heeled, birds pattering

wet pavement. I wanted to be color but in the end was

swallowed by bedlam, a calm in blue yesterday's panic was not wasted

An escape is an endless waltz pending

a mother feeds blue candies to a baby

To say it by mouth is simpler

but the hand is more accurate

Though one could not write herself out of time

or power. Lids were drawn against skies

Even if minutes brought nothing to read

I want to trace every one of your lines

I've never been to the spot but I trust you to guide me

Investigating the many paths to misery

Rolling out leaves, mistaking grammar for

gramophone, a correspondence proceeds

by way of etymology. We don't go forward

determining meaning but back into the word

Fragrance of a lure trembling

a shudder feeds blue alleys to a maybe

Fair ringing air, air foreign, air faring

First I set out to admire your reflection, second

to love, encourage and be rid of you. Then I sought

to beg, barter and betray. I kissed what it was like

to want only what was given, each perfect breath

After our epic feign tide I wrote steadily opaque

What I wanted to say but could not: I trust you know

An amulet links bodies in time, viscosity

You beside me, a fiction

Listening to unlatched valves inside the poem

Wind, rain and leaves blew up

earlier than air

Hands are cold and hair alights to clouds

Bare wringing air, air florid, air staring

Laynie Brown

CONTRIBUTORS

Emily Abendroth is a poet, teacher and anti-prison activist living in Philadelphia. Her published works include the poetry book *]Exclosures[* and *The Instead*, a collaborative book with fiction writer Miranda Mellis, as well as numerous chapbooks. She has been awarded a Pew Fellowship in Poetry and residencies at the MacDowell Colony, the Millay Colony, and the Headlands Center for the Arts.

Laynie Browne is a poet, prose writer, teacher and editor. She is author of thirteen collections of poems and three novels. Her most recent collections of poems include *You Envelop Me* (Omnidawn 2017) **P R A C T I C E** (SplitLevel 2015), and *Scorpyn Odes* (Kore Press 2015) Her honors include a 2014 Pew Fellowship, the National Poetry Series Award (2007) for her collection *The Scented Fox*, selected by Alice Notley, and the Contemporary Poetry Series Award (2005) for her collection *Drawing of a Swan Before Memory*. Her poetry has been translated into French, Spanish, Chinese and Catalan and has appeared in many anthologies including *The Norton Anthology of Post Modern Poetry* (second edition 2013), *Ecopoetry: A Contemporary American Anthology* (Trinity University Press, 2013), *Bay Poetics* (Faux Press, 2006) and *The Reality Street Book of Sonnets* (Reality Street, 2008). Her critical writing has appeared in journals including *Jacket2, Aufgabe , Open Letter* and *Talisman*. She co-edited *I'll Drown My Book: Conceptual Writing by Women* (Les Figues Press, 2012) and is currently editing an anthology of original essays on the Poet's Novel. She teaches at University of Pennsylvania and at Swarthmore College.

Maryan Nagy Captan is an Egyptian-American poet and performer living in Philadelphia, where she serves as Art Director at *Apiary Magazine* and teaches experimental and experiential writing classes at The Head & The Hand Press. Her first collection, *copy/body*, was published by Empty Set Press in June 2017. Her poetry can be found in *Mad House, AJAR, APIARY* Magazine and *CRED* Magazine.

Kate Colby's seventh book of poetry, *The Arrangements*, is forthcoming from Four Way Books in 2018. She has received awards and fellowships from Harvard's Woodberry Poetry Room, the Poetry Society of America and Rhode Island State Council for the Arts. She lives and works as a copywriter in Providence.

Marissa Johnson-Valenzuela was born and raised in Wichita, Kansas and, though she's also paid some sort of rent in Lawrence, Detroit, D.C., Laramie, Havana and the Mexican state of Chiapas, a collective house in Philadelphia has long been home. Her writing has been supported by many rad people and projects including *Organize Your Own: The Politics and Poetics of Self-Determination Movements* (Soberscove 2016). She is the founder of Thread Makes Blanket press and teaches at Community College of Philadelphia.

Emma Brown Sanders is a queer Philly poet from Chicago. She runs POETRY JAWNS: a podcast with Alina Pleskova. Her work can be found in Fungiculture, Bedfellows, Recreation League, and the tiny.

Davy Knittle is the author of the chapbooks 'empathy for cars / force of july' (horse less press) and 'cyclorama' (the operating system). His poems and reviews have appeared recently in *The Recluse, Fence, Jacket2*, and *Sixth Finch*. He lives in Philadelphia where he curates the City Planning Poetics series at the Kelly Writers House.

Michael Leong is the author of *e.s.p.* (Silenced Press, 2009), *Cutting Time with a Knife* (Black Square Editions, 2012), and *Who Unfolded My Origami Brain?* (Fence Digital, 2017). His poetry has appeared or is forthcoming in *The &NOW AWARDS 2: The Best Innovative Writing and Best American Experimental Writing 2018*. He is Assistant Professor of English at the University at Albany, SUNY.

Chris Schaeffer is a PhD candidate at Temple University researching Spiritualist poetics. Previous work has appeared in *Bedfellows, Industrial Lunch, Animal Kingdom, The Volta*, and elsewhere. Previous chapbooks extraordinarily out of print and buried in the earth.

Mai Schwartz is a poet, a storyteller, a teacher, a gardener, and a native of New Jersey with lots of opinions about diners and malls. In 2015, Mai was declared 'officially awesome' by Philly karaoke legend Dr. Thunder and has the papers to prove it.

R/B Mertz is a genderqueer/dyke artist & poet & writing teacher, a Christian homeschooler gone wrong. New poems are coming out in *The Gay and Lesbian Review, Fence, Pittsburgh Poetry Review, Whiskey & Fox,* and old poems in assorted elsewheres, such as *DIAGRAM, Drunken Boat,* and *MAYDAY;* her art is currently hanging in Maryland, Pennsylvania, Ohio, California, Florida, New York, and West Virginia. She's writing a memoir entitled Burning Butch. Mertz is 32, which surpasses expectations.

This text was set in 11pt Baskerville, a serif typeface designed in 1757 by John Baskerville (1706–1775). Typesetting and design by Levi Bentley.